To my Mother
who is a continuous source
of inspiration,
and to
my first grandchild
Natasha

Merry Mischief

Lost in time
This childhood past
Memories in gold are cast

ACKNOWLEDGMENTS

The author and publishers wish to thank

Clarence House
The Archivists Windsor Castle
The National Portrait Gallery
The British Library
The Nottingham Library
The Victoria and Albert Museum
Westminster Cathedral
Holy Trinity Sloane Street
The National Railway Museum
The London Transport Museum

FIRST PUBLISHED IN THE UNITED KINGDOM 2001 BY LEPPI PUBLICATIONS
BRITISH LIBRARY CATALOGUING IN PUBLICATION DATA
Merry Mischief
Copyright © 2001 Leppi Publications - Savonarola Editoriale Inc
ISBN 0-9521644-3

Leppi Publications
PO Box 3278, 805 Finchley Road
London NW11 8DP United Kingdom

Merry Mischief

celebrating the childhood of Her Majesty Queen Elizabeth The Queen Mother

the story of the little girl

Elizabeth Bowes Lyon

who would become Queen one day

Marialuisa Marino

ACKNOWLEDGMENTS

The author wishes to thank her Majesty Queen Elizabeth the Queen Mother for her gracious permission to reproduce the portrait commissioned by Sir Malcolm Arnold for Her Majesty's one hundredth birthday celebration. Her Majesty's kindness has inspired me to continue in my chosen artistic path.

My grateful thanks to Sir Alastair Aird, Queen Elizabeth the Queen Mother's private secretary for his enormous encouragement and help in believing that my book would be a delightful introduction to Her Majesty's early childhood days.

My special thanks to Sir Malcolm Arnold, who commissioned Her Majesty's portrait for her birthday celebration.

This book could not have come about without my publisher, Leppi Publications, to whom I am deeply indebted.

To Marco Houston for editing this book and having it published in time to celebrate Queen Elizabeth The Queen Mother's one hundred and first birthday.

To my three sons who while watching them grow up gave me the greatest pleasure, and to all my family and friends far and wide for their constant support.

I wish to thank the following people for their help and encouragement; His Excellency the Italian Ambassador Luigi Amaduzzi, Peter Beales for the Elizabeth of Glamis Rose image, The Scotch House, Massimo Marino for photography, Tanja Petrushevski, Judy Widmann-Pederneski, Anthony John Day, Richard Taylor, Nevil Rogers and all those who contributed and generously gave their time toward the publication.

Introduction

The Happy Childhood Memories
Of Her Majesty Queen Elizabeth The Queen Mother
Creating Cameo Events Of Her Life.

A nostalgic Edwardian childhood holds a treasury of illuminating chapters . . .

With a message in the image of innocence, the magical qualities of this little girl touched many hearts in the delight of her company.

Little Elizabeth had a tender and sensible nature, growing up with the joys of the open countryside and the pleasures of the city, allowing her to develop her ingenuity, properly educated, with impeccable manners.

The cultivation of fruit and flowers was her delight, noble habits of early rising, order and neatness, passion of benevolence, the Bible and Psalms. A natural little lass, fun loving, delightfully mischievous but wise.
She was naughty but nice.

A ray of sunshine on a gloomy day.

Happy in the world of make believe.

Everyone should be free to follow one's dream no matter what.

In the world of fairy tales the beautiful heroine and the handsome prince fall in love and live happily ever after.

The story I wish to tell you is true in its history, adding a touch of fantasy with a blend of reality. The exciting events that befall Elizabeth have the fabric that legends are built on.

The beautiful Elizabeth, with shiny, long, dark locks, wild rose skin, eyes of celtic sapphire blue and a radiating charm that could win the heart of a prince.

Albert was enchanted with Elizabeth when the two children met at the birthday party in London. The destinies of two lives were bonded, kept preciously alive to unite many years later when Prince Albert would fall in love with the beautiful young Duchess Elizabeth.

Queen Elizabeth The Queen Mother has captured my heart. I delved into the Edwardian world, imagined I was there . . . Elizabeth could have been my best friend, and I am sure you will feel the same as you read what a lovely, fun loving mischievous little girl she was. Yet with a good sense of right and wrong, willing to please her mother and father who supported her exquisite little character.

The fairy tale is true . . . you know . . . if you wish . . . who knows . . . maybe your wildest dreams can come true.

Marialuisa Marino

Merry Mischief

The story of Elizabeth Bowes Lyon
The little girl who would become Queen one day.

4th August 2001

Dear Miss Marino

Queen Elizabeth The Queen Mother has asked me to write and thank you so much for your birthday greetings and gift.

The Queen Mother much appreciated your thought in giving Her Majesty this beautifully illustrated manuscript in such a splendid cover. Queen Elizabeth accepts your present with feelings of great pleasure.

Yours sincerely

Private Secretary to
Queen Elizabeth The Queen Mother

Miss Marialuisa Marino

Queen Elizabeth The Queen Mother

Portrait of Her Majesty Queen ELizabeth The Queen Mother
Commissioned by Sir Malcolm Arnold CBE to celebrate H.M. 100th Birthday
on August 4th 2000
By Prof. Marialuisa Marino

Contents

Do you believe in fairies?
This is the fairy tale of the century.

Elizabeth Bowes Lyon born into a family both ancient and grand.

A Lady, a Duchess, a Queen

Her family motto was clear and precise

'In thee, my God, I place my trust without change to the end.'

Through The Eyes Of A Child

Elizabeth found herself enchanted
and closely in touch with a fantasy world
she created for herself and her brother.

Family Tree

Elizabeth had royal blood, being a descendant of Robert the Bruce, King of the Scots. Her family name is Bowes-Lyon. 'The White Lyon'; blond Sir John Lyons had been given Glamis Castle on the edge of the Highlands by King Robert II of Scotland in 1372.

Sir John Lyon was keeper of the Privy Seal, he married Princess Joan, daughter of King Robert II and became Thane and the first Lord of Glamis.

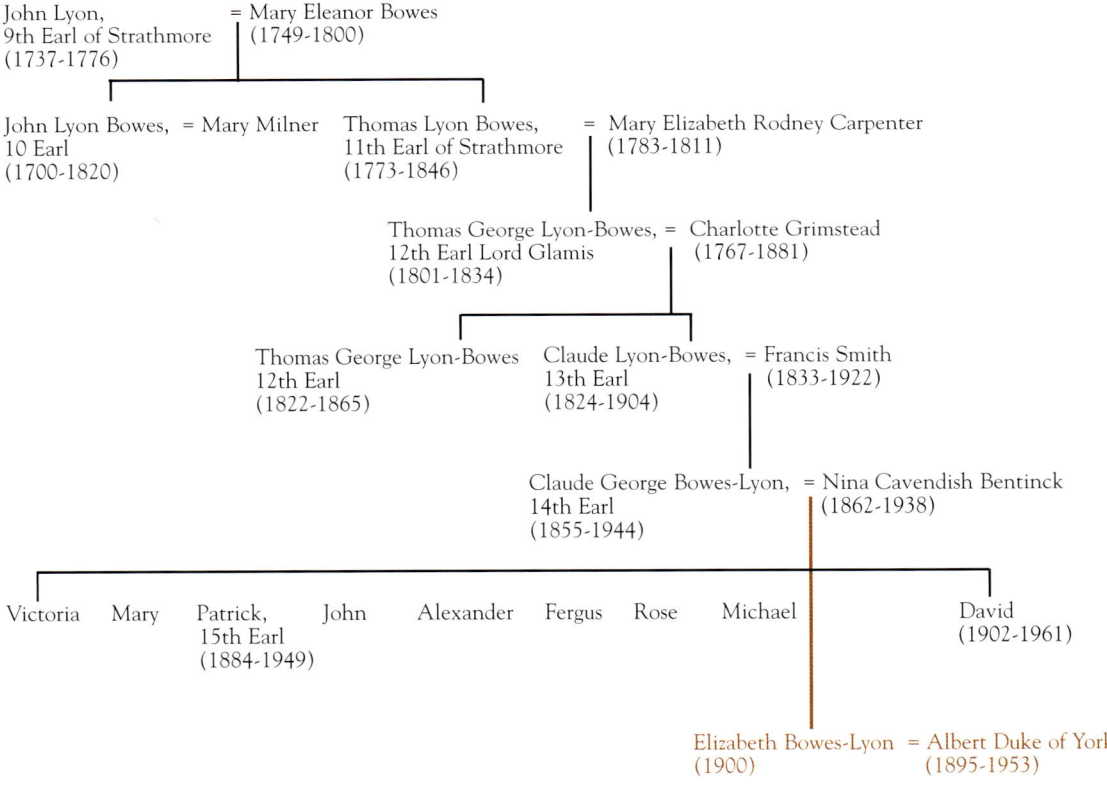

John Lyon,
9th Earl of Strathmore
(1737-1776)
= Mary Eleanor Bowes
(1749-1800)

John Lyon Bowes,
10 Earl
(1700-1820)
= Mary Milner

Thomas Lyon Bowes,
11th Earl of Strathmore
(1773-1846)
= Mary Elizabeth Rodney Carpenter
(1783-1811)

Thomas George Lyon-Bowes,
12th Earl Lord Glamis
(1801-1834)
= Charlotte Grimstead
(1767-1881)

Thomas George Lyon-Bowes
12th Earl
(1822-1865)

Claude Lyon-Bowes,
13th Earl
(1824-1904)
= Francis Smith
(1833-1922)

Claude George Bowes-Lyon,
14th Earl
(1855-1944)
= Nina Cavendish Bentinck
(1862-1938)

Victoria   Mary   Patrick,
15th Earl
(1884-1949)
John   Alexander   Fergus   Rose   Michael   David
(1902-1961)

Elizabeth Bowes-Lyon
(1900)
= Albert Duke of York
(1895-1953)

Following the abdication of his brother, Edward VIII, on 10th December 1936, Albert became George VI King of England and Elizabeth became his Queen.

3

mariacruisa marino.

Family Life, Past & Present

SCOTLAND

Glamis Castle

NORTHERN IRELAND

ENGLAND

MARIALUISA

St Paul's Walden Bury

Once upon a time and far away, the beautiful castle of Glamis set in the Tayside hills of Scotland

and the country house in the Hertfordshire hamlet of St Paul's Walden Bury

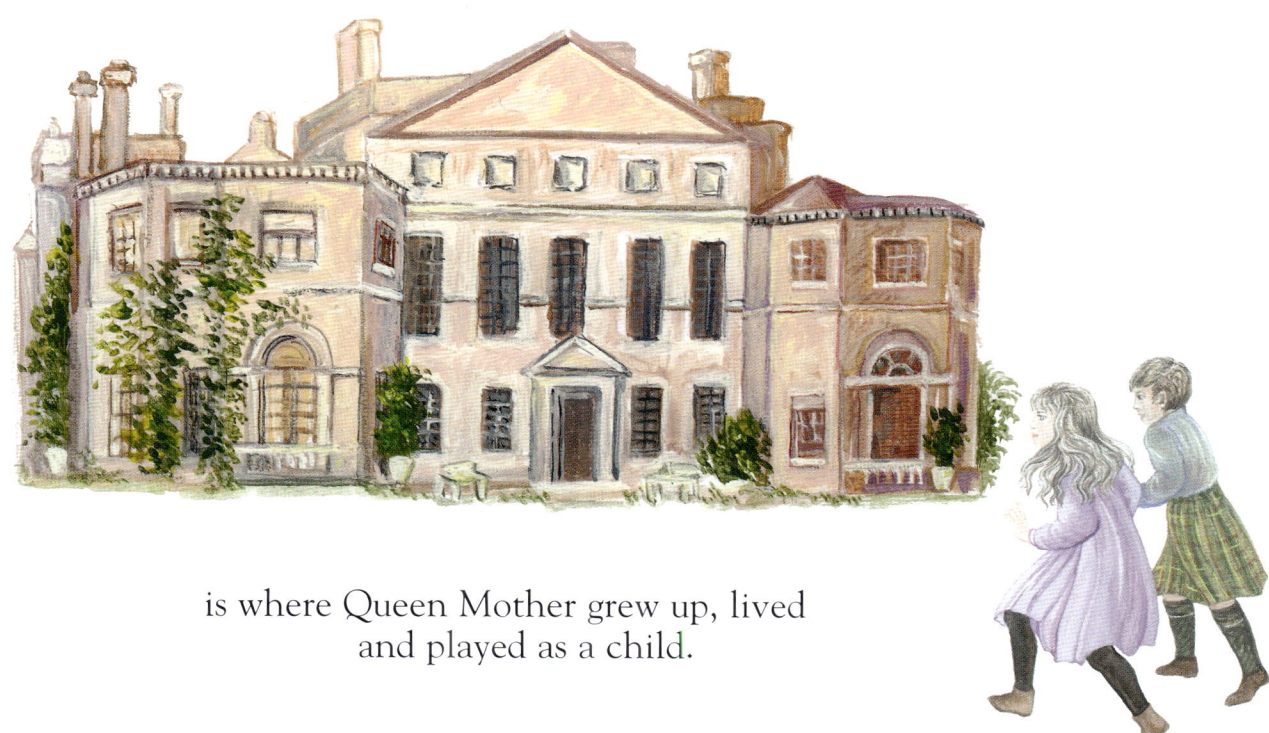

is where Queen Mother grew up, lived and played as a child.

Elizabeth Angela Marguerite Bowes Lyon

On the 4th of August 1900 Elizabeth was born to one of the oldest and most distinguished families in Scotland. She is the youngest daughter of the 14th Earl and Countess of Strathmore and Kinghorn, and the ninth of ten children . . . Violet, who died aged fourteen from diphtheria; May, who was seventeen when Elizabeth was born; followed by Patrick, Jock, Alexander, Fergus, Rose and Michael.

When Elizabeth was twenty one months old, David was born. The clan was happy and down to earth.

Nina Cecilia Cavendish Bentinck

This family could not have had a more wonderful, talented and artistic mother, never needing to punish them, but gently showing them the right way.

She was a descendant of the Duke of Portland, Prime Minister to King George III.

'Duty is the rent you pay for life' was one of her favourite sayings, a motto that Elizabeth would carry with her for the rest of her life. Religion was very important for her and this faith extended into her daily life.

She was admired and adored by all her children.

Elizabeth's sweet-natured but absent-minded father was six weeks late in registering her birth. Although she was born in London, her father recorded her arrival at the nearby Bury in Hitchin two days before her christening.

Claud George Bowes-Lyon, 14th Earl of Strathmore and 22nd Baron of Glamis

Lady Strathmore made sure her children would be introduced to the refinement of good taste, to learn and appreciate beautiful paintings and lovely furniture in the Edwardian lifestyle, bringing artistic grace to life, yet to be wise enough, run free and enjoy the wonderful vast countryside.

Since 1882 Grandmother, Mrs Harry Scott, had lived high in the hills of Florence. Elizabeth and her brother David were escorted to Italy by their spinster aunt, Violet.

Mrs Scott divided her time between her English home, Forbes House near Ham Common in London, and the Villa Capponi at Fiesole.

Italy made an incredible impression on the young Elizabeth, and Lady Strathmore brought a touch of Tuscany to Glamis Castle, creating the Italian garden. Elizabeth's passion for horticulture was never to leave her.

Family Circle

There was contentment in this big family circle. Family friends would visit this happy household year after year.

The Strathmores divided their time between their three properties, St Paul's Walden Bury in Hertfordshire, part of the time in St James's Square, London, and Glamis Castle in Scotland.

Summer Holidays

Usually three months of the summer holidays were spent at Glamis Castle. There were dinners by candlelight and the guests would be entertained in the great oak-panelled dining room.

With the two pipers in their elegant kilts, marching around the table.

On some occasions Elizabeth would be allowed to come down from her room to join the guests at the grand table for dessert.

Elizabeth's father was a good sportsman and excellent cricketer. Lord Strathmore shared his wife's passion for music, he loved to recite the classics and was an expert on the Bible.

Beyond the woods and moors the older members would shoot for grouse and woodcock. Salmon fishing on the River Tay was a great pastime sport for the guests. Many a visitor would come away with happy memories of time spent with the Strathmores at Glamis.

Mother was a highly talented musician. There was dancing and singing, and the Countess of Strathmore played the piano on many occasions. The family played games and charades in the Great Hall.

The noblest sound is music
the inspiration of the soul.

Floating gently across the air
enchantment in control.

The flow of angels voices
the Devil's darker toll.

Life transcending changing
moods versatile and whole.

12

Young Elizabeth had the best of both worlds; her mother's enthusiasm and exquisite taste and her father's down to earth character.

Elizabeth and David were inseparable and were nicknamed, from the bible, my 'two Benjamins', by their mother.

Despite Mother's protests Elizabeth was so full of fun, that she was lovingly called 'Merry Mischief' but her brother could only manage "Elizabuff".

Later in life she would be called 'Buffy' to her close circle of family and friends.

Destined to achieve greatness Queen Elizabeth the Queen Mother was to reach her one hundredth year with bravery, determination, and in difficult moments, with an infinite sense of optimism, with qualities of courage, dutifulness and grace attributed to a great lady.

Elizabeth was to win the affection of the British People in supporting her nervous but sensitive husband, the future King George VI in 1936.

The Queen Mother's sense of fun and laughter makes her a very special person. She has been a supportive wife to one sovereign, King George VI, and Queen Mother to another sovereign, Elizabeth II.

A person with such enthusiasm, shaping the direction and fashion of the monarchy, at the same time Queen Mother has inspired the nation with her down to earth nature reaching out to thousands of admirers worldwide with her magic and charm.

When Elizabeth was born Queen Victoria was still alive, aged eighty one, and living at Buckingham Palace. The great monarch, who gave her name to the nineteenth century, passed away on 22nd January 1901.

England In April

I walk the path of deepened early April mist in vain,
and have not seen yet a single drop of rain.

England's weather did history make,
in two hundred years has not been seen
so dry an April heat and sun awake.

The land breathes sorrow, dusty air,
beyond dry woods leap fox and hare.

A scattered wilderness where beasts now need
the help of human hand
where spiral winds are dancing with arid sand.

The trickling stream has now lost her way,
and the river shallow, has no undulating wave to play.

The glimmering water, the sun greedily drinks dry,
and at sunset there is not a shadow of a cloud in the sky.

And the moon looks down on man's harvest overthrown,
on dry land of thirsty rows of seeds already sown.

It seems as if nature's twist uncontrolled runs wild,
bathing in her frolic, gambling with man like a
mischievous and naughty child.

Playfully overlooks her harmony in frail
and perishable state,
forgets to weep those tears of joy ruins her life's
fountains in a dizzy fleeting rate.

Risking an unrewarding toilsome journey,
now treacherously long,
man challenges her capers,
and her capricious April song.

Out Of This World
Time Traveller

MARIALUISA MARINO.

From our very own 'Out Of This World Time traveller'... sit back in your seat... go back into the veiled mist of yesteryear... and you will miraculously synchronise with 'Out Of Time'... to the most exciting days in the childhood life of a little girl called Elizabeth.

We *are transported to an England where the clock is ticking back a century where our 'Out of this World Timetraveler'*

Stops!

The story unfolds.
Through our looking glass
we see an Edwardian World.
You are no longer in the year 2001.

It is not difficult to imagine Elizabeth's natural joy
while she plays happily with her brother David
in a most beautiful garden.

18

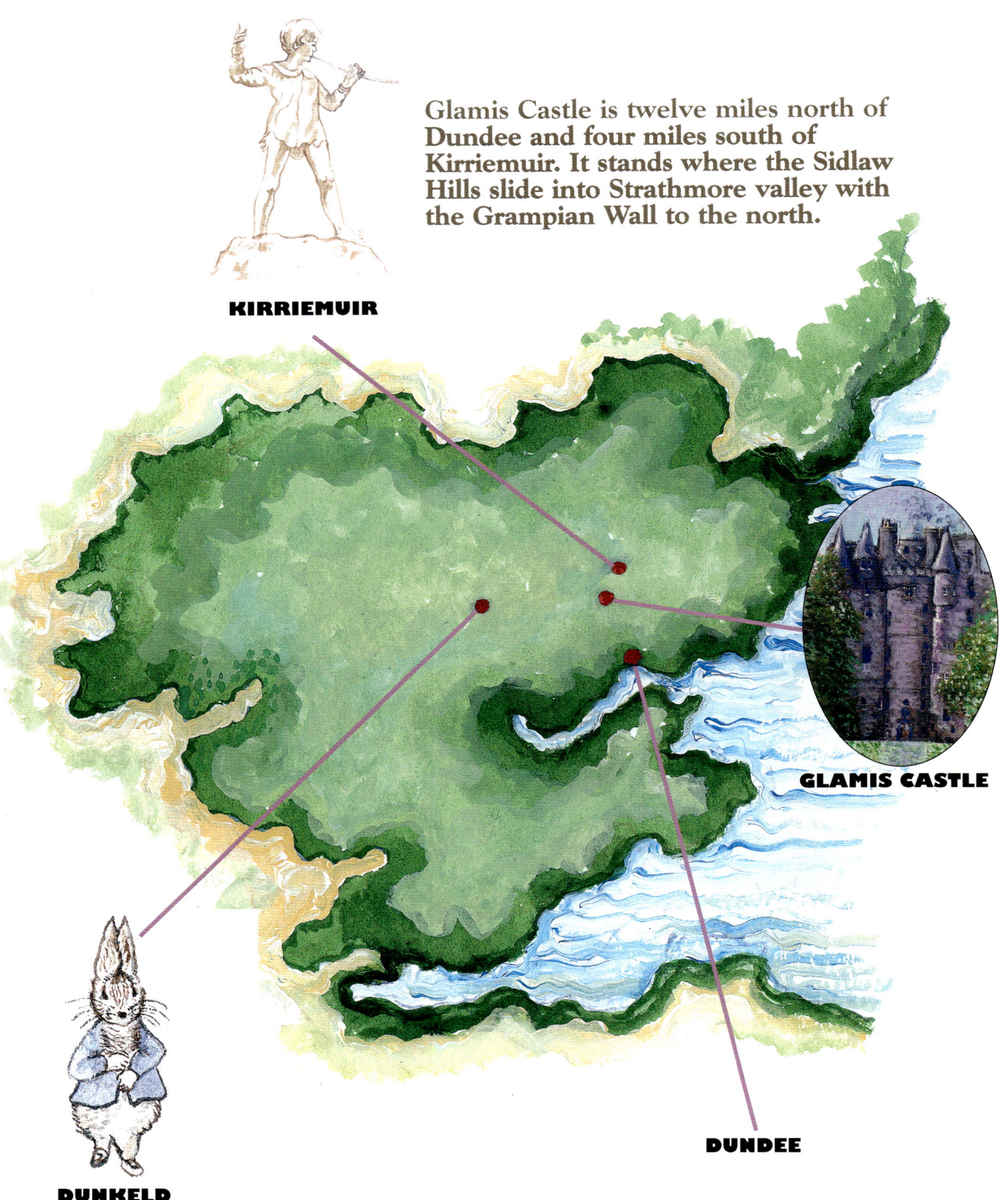

Glamis Castle is twelve miles north of Dundee and four miles south of Kirriemuir. It stands where the Sidlaw Hills slide into Strathmore valley with the Grampian Wall to the north.

KIRRIEMUIR

GLAMIS CASTLE

DUNDEE

DUNKELD

19

Angus

The 'Time Traveller' is lingering over the Angus coastline with its rocky bays and red sandstone cliffs. As we approach the beautiful heather covered hills and glens, in the distance we see the castle of Glamis. Between mountain and sea is the most spectacular view . . .

Do you know that Beatrix Potter spent many holidays as a child not far away from here, near Dunkeld. Peter Rabbit and Jemima Puddleduck, I am sure, are running about the woods, and in Kirriemuir where J.M. Barrie was born . . . you know . . . Peter Pan, the boy who wouldn't grow up, is flying there . . . somewhere.

When we imagine . . . we escape into the timeless zone . . . where age does not count . . . but . . . what we feel in our hearts never grows old.

The Thirteenth Earl's Golden Wedding Ceremony

28 September 1903

Elizabeth's earliest recollection

Sitting on her grandfather's knee, looking out of the beautiful castle window she remembers colourful lights, the whole park was lit in the evening by Chinese lanterns and padella lights.

In the ancestral castle of Glamis when the thirteenth Earl's golden wedding ceremony took place, the Scottish heritage was grand to see. Pipes were played and Mr Neill's string quartet entertained the guests at the party, creating a delightful atmosphere.

The grandchildren were all there to present a gift – a magnificent grandfather clock, listing twenty seven names engraved on the dial.

Six hundred guests came to tea and join the festivities which extended well into the late hours for three days and three nights.

*Glamis Castle is set in the gentle hills
below the Grampian Highlands.*

22

Beyond Fantasy

Out of the prison of consciousness
living fantasy springs in the mind's eye.

We are part of fleeting moments,
beyond fantasy we are free to fly.

And in this transient moment,
we dance on the winds of time.

An infinite flow of inventions
revolving in one's mind.

We then become the fantasy,
maybe real or fairy tale.

Thus from one's heart
we muse and dream

then we gently sail.

And in the pleasure of living,
in this creative space

We have created art,
for the future human race.

Children's Heaven

Our 'Out Of This World Time Traveller' brings us to the South of England . . . We stop . . . at the edge of the enchanted woods, we have a vast view in front of us . . . imagine . . . the soft fragrant air of the countryside and the gentle breeze on our faces gives us a sense of well being and serenity.

Honeysuckle & Magnolia

We are in Hertfordshire, in the rambling estate and spaciousness of the country house of St Paul's Walden Bury. Imagine an elegant Queen Anne mansion, with its red brick exterior, covered in honey-suckle and magnolia giving an exquisite aroma in the air. This is where Elizabeth and her family's early days were spent. The elegant home was built by the fine architect Sir William Chambers.

Though a little worn, the house had a warm and loving family atmosphere. With the dogs, Persian cats, rabbits, and tortoises, Elizabeth and David had no time to get bored.

The house is set on a rise surrounded by lush green lawns and woodlands. A harness room and stables, the tumbledown barn, a giant oak, alleys ending with statues, hawthorn clipped to shapes, recall an influence of Andre le Notre, the great designer of the Versailles gardens in France. There were yew hedges, rock gardens, roses, mulberries, limes, strawberries and more.

*St Paul's Walden Bury is set
deep in the heart of the Hertfordshire countryside*

The Enchanted Woods

The ponds, lakes and hidden statues are Elizabeth's special delights.

Elizabeth cries out "David, David! . . Let's run to the woods, to the statue of the discus thrower, he does look like a butler, doesn't he?"

David observed the statue's resemblance and looked up at his sister and said,

"Yes look, he delivered all the drinks but he still has the tray."

"David, bring out your sword so we can give him a royal ceremony and knight him The Bounding Butler."

"I Elizabeth dub you The Bounding Butler"

After having so much fun with the ceremony which Elizabeth loved to perform, they ran back to the main house for tea.

In the farmland haymaking was fun, "it makes you very hot in the sun, but there is a delicious smell in the fields," Elizabeth recalls.

Then the breeze came up to brush you gently on your face to cool you down.

At about six o'clock Elizabeth would run to the harness room to get Bantam eggs for tea.

Elizabeth would feed the hens early in the morning and some of the animals would loyally follow her around, whilst she checked to see that no ravenous foxes would hurt her hens during the night.

Elizabeth would not forget to feed the two splendid pigs, black Berkshires named Emma and Lucifer. They were intelligent and would eagerly wait for Elizabeth to bring them ripe red apples.

Two Ring-Doves

The path of fairyland,
In the enchanted woods,
At the bottom of the garden,
Where the tall trees stood.

Under the shade of the big oak tree,
Two ring doves,
Are flying free.

Caroline Curley-Love,
and Rhoda Wrigley-Worm,
Fly to Elizabeth,
Each in turn.

Then into the wicker cage,
at the end of each day,
the two gentle doves
would not fly away.

The Nursery

Would you like to play with Elizabeth and her brother? The Time Traveller brings us into the sunny nursery . . .

Come in . . . and join us . . .

30

Clara Cooper Knight, the daughter of a farmer, was their nursery-maid. Elizabeth and David called her 'Allah', close enough to pronouncing 'Clara'. Her ever watchful, comforting presence created a very happy atmosphere in the nursery. The walls of the nursery were adorned with favourite story pictures that were framed and hung up by the gardener, twenty years before.

"All good things come to an end . . . say your prayers properly and don't mumble, you're talking to God . . . off to bed . . . good night!" was Clara's way of teaching the two little ones.

The nursery was full of toys from the past . . . though handed down they were no less loved because they had signs of wear.

Christmas toys . . . birthday toys . . . and new toys . . . Dolls . . . Dolls houses . . . rocking horse . . . toy soldiers . . . bears . . . balls . . . hoops . . . cards . . . dominoes and many games.

Elizabeth loved dolls but they had to have eyes that opened and shut.

She loved flowers too, so it was fun calling her dolls Rose and Poppy. There were very little dolls, shabby but loved, dolls that belonged to her sisters and a big doll that would cry if you turned her over.

"Mama" Rose would cry.

Poppy was pretty too, but could do nothing at all, except open and shut her eyes. Her lashes and hair were real and Elizabeth loved to brush her hair into different styles and tie it with many coloured satin ribbons.

Picnic under the Oak tree

It's a beautiful sunny day.

"I'm going to take you all for a picnic under the oak tree", Elizabeth spoke to her dolls as though she was their mother. She gathered the dolls into her arms and asked David to bring the rug and tea cups. David did this, but he put all his toy tin soldiers into the cups.

They walked across the garden towards the oak tree. By then all the family pets were following behind the two. Bobs, her pony, the dogs and the cats.

When the procession reached the oak tree, to their surprise, there was a little yellow duckling waddling around the rugged brown trunk.

Elizabeth cried "Oh dear! The little fluffy duckling is lost!" They all observed the duckling in a curious manner, all of a sudden mother duck came towards Elizabeth. "Quack, Quack" she nudged the duckling away towards the other youngsters.

"Even mother ducks want you to go back home, they get rather anxious, just like daddies and mummies do!" Elizabeth exclaimed.

"Do you remember, Elizabuff, when you climbed the apple tree in the orchard and mummy said you should not go bird nesting again?"

"Well . . . the mummy duck makes her nursery high up in the trees" Elizabeth said in an assertive manner. "And the ducklings come down from the nest, isn't it funny David!"

"That's a wild duck" she explained. Her father, Lord Strathmore, taught her a lot about the woodland wildlife.

They sat under the oak tree and Elizabeth talked and talked about adventures. She poured tea for her dolls while David was systematically shooting his tin soldiers down one by one.

"Of course . . . David . . . you can't always agree . . . but it is a little silly shooting soldiers while we are having tea."

"I know about that!" David said. "I'm not bothered about playing with your dolls, lets play something else."

Running hurriedly towards the stables Elizabeth spotted a tiny bird, half-hidden in the high grass; "Oh look David! The foxes have killed a little bird." David felt very sad to see this little feathered friend lying motionless in the field.

"We have to give it an official burial, and we shall have to be quite quick, before Allah catches us out here before breakfast."

Elizabeth ran into the playroom to fetch a little box, then picking pink roses from the garden, carefully placed each petal in the box where the dead bird would rest. By then David had dug up some sand, and together they buried the little bird.

This is truly the angelic side of Elizabeth's nature. Her love and tender care for animals showed the feminine side of her normally mischievious tomboy behaviour.

Engrossed in the burial of the little bird, Clara Copper Knight's voice was only heard at a distance by the little sister and brother. They had no problem with this as Allah, their devoted nurse maid was strict but kind.

"Look at the pair of you" Allah called out. "I think you'd better come into the house and wash up, it's almost time for tea."

Elizabeth's wonderful companions, her little brown spaniel, Peter, and Buffy the tabby cat ran after them.

It was always alright with Allah, and the two little ones clapped their hands and tea was welcomed.

34

Butterflies

When the wings of butterflies flutter about,
After a light spring shower.

Dancing on the breeze in the bright sunlight,
spreading gold dust from flower to flower.

Bobs

Bobs

St Paul's
Walden Bury
1906

Our 'Out Of This World Time Traveller' is following the gentle contour of the green hills. We are approaching the outhouses of Walden Bury, where we see Bobs venturing out of his stable and galloping toward the house. Elizabeth is trying to catch him before he reaches the front door.

Bobs, Ever Faithful

The Shetland pony is the smallest of all the breeds of ponies. It has faced rather more danger than most animals in being treated as a toy, but having a very sensitive and loyal nature it is especially good as a family pet and particularly so for children.

Bobs was given to Elizabeth at the age of three. This beautiful dark brown Shetland pony had a soft summer fur and a shiny silky winter coat. Bobs had an amazing abundant flowing mane, forelock and tail.

Trained well to perform in harness, Bobs had a friendly nature and, like a large dog, would follow Elizabeth wherever she went. Out on the fields and into the house . . . and up the stairs!

This was a favourite game, as a certain amount of flexibility was encouraged by her down to earth father.

"Bobs" cried Elizabeth,

"Don't be so naughty, mother might not be quite so happy to see you following me up the stairs."

"David, . . . quick . . . help me take Bobs outside". Bobs rolled his eyes and laid back his ears . . . "this could be trouble", thought Elizabeth. But she knew how to handle him, and so, to calm him down, she gave him a lump of sugar she always kept tucked away in her pocket.

Dressed in her red riding habit, she would ride Bobs confidently tearing around the estate.

Owning a pony was a responsibility, but great fun, Bobs was quite tame because Elizabeth understood the pony's sensitivity. Taking him back to the groom she would help rub him down, talking the whole time.

She was a chatter box!

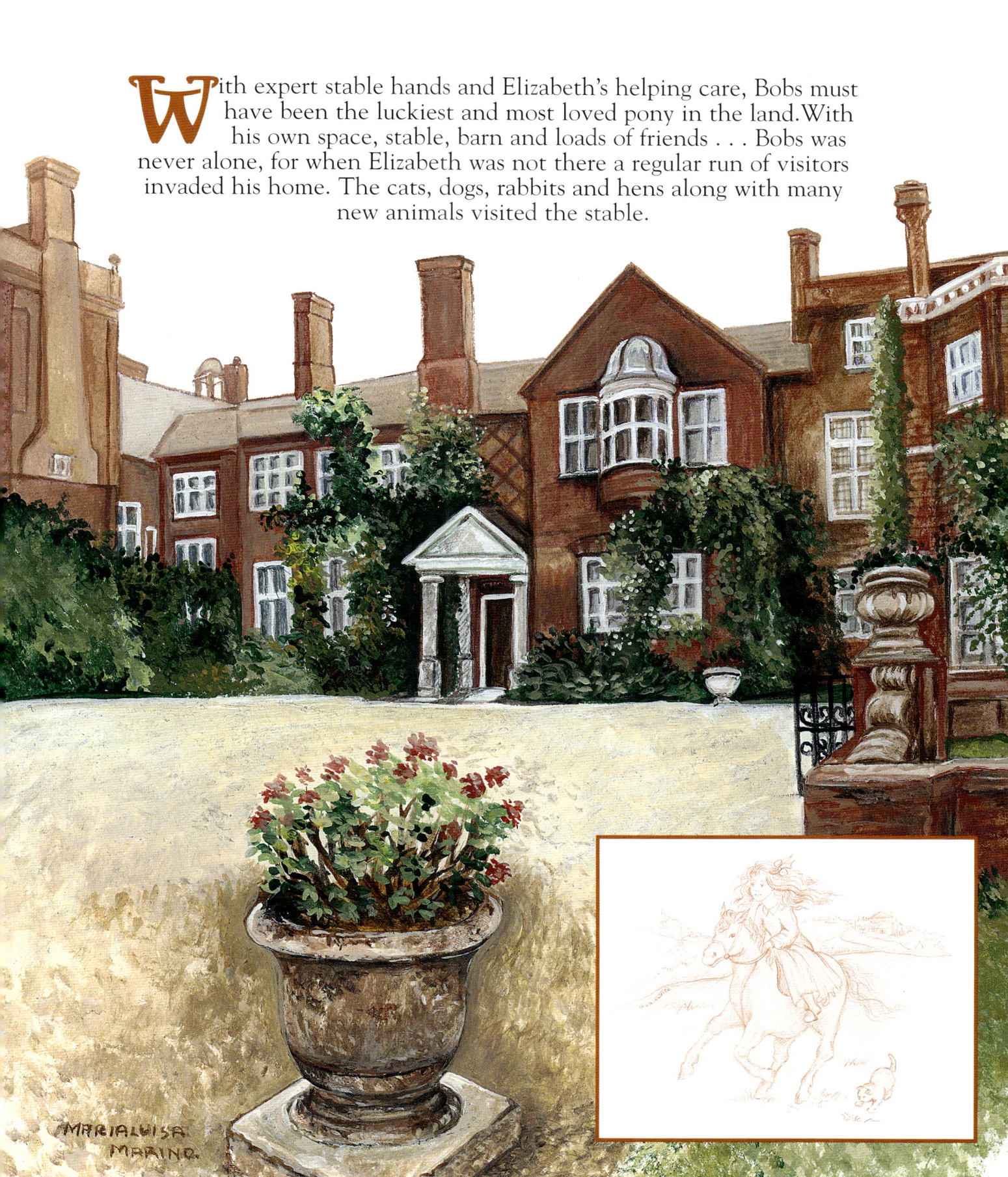

With expert stable hands and Elizabeth's helping care, Bobs must have been the luckiest and most loved pony in the land. With his own space, stable, barn and loads of friends . . . Bobs was never alone, for when Elizabeth was not there a regular run of visitors invaded his home. The cats, dogs, rabbits and hens along with many new animals visited the stable.

MARIALUISA
MARINO.

Elizabeth was very confident and learned to ride Bobs well, and they bonded together like two old friends. This particular morning Elizabeth was in high spirits, it was a fine day, she ran through the fields. The dew drops were shining against the rising sun reflecting white specks from the daisies scattered all over the green grass.

In the early hours the birds were noisily flying about, this was a great day to ride Bobs.

With David not far behind, Merry Mischief approached the barn,

"Oh no! . . Look! The barn door is wide open, where is Bobs?" Elizabeth said concerned. But then her beloved little dog, Peter, was not around . . . nor Buffy the tabby cat . . . or the rabbits.

Elizabeth took David by the hand as they ran over the gentle slope of the hill. There they found all the animals dancing and romping happily in a wide circle.

This was a very beautiful sight to see.

Child Of The Universe

I am a child of the universe,
so take me by the hand,
I am spirit inspiration,
I reflect in all things grand.

I am present in all four seasons,
for I am nature's child.
A vortex in all four winds.
I am chaos I am wild.

Don't look for me when I am gone,
in the anger of the storm.
In transitory darkness,
deepest shadows will transform.

The perfect day will be at hand,
to pass the gloom away.
The dawn of light a wonderland,
where nature's colours play.

The bluest sky, white mountain peaks,
green fields and golden sand.
I dip myself in nature's paint,
create a picture grand.

I wonder through sweet
scented fields,

with intoxicating passion.
This mind blowing flowering
countryside,
changes essence into fashion.

I am that timeless child of nature,
so please take me by the hand.
I hold all secrets of the universe,
for you to understand.

40

The Fairy Queen's Birthday

High up in a tree there are fairies
Beyond the hills . . . there are elves
Pixies, goblins and little people,
Are merrily enjoying themselves.

They ring silver and blue bells to make music
And sit on mushrooms . . . fairy rings,
They dance on the dewy grass
And ride on little bird's wings.

Glow-worms stand in a row . . . for fine lanterns
The stars lend their light for the summer ball
The Fairy King sends out invitations
To all citizens, be they big . . . or small . . .

The Fairy folk are extremely excited,
For the Fairy Queen's birthday shall be grand
Good news spreads far and wide
From the enchanted forest to the magical woodland

If you have the red seal and crown invitation
You can queue at the palace door
Drink dew-drops flavoured with orange juice
And dance on the "disco" floor

Naughty goblins, ogres or gremlins,
Would not be invited to the banquet of dreams
"Come true dreams" and "midnight rings"

Invitation is only . . . for good children it seems!

Fairies

The 'Time traveller' stops . . . on its magical path right in the middle of fairy land, where field fairies ride on the back of butterfly wings, flowers and

Fairies

St Paul's
Walden Bury
1906

mushrooms
are full of . . .
little pixies
and elves.
Laughing,
chatting and
singing . . .

42

Fairies

Elizabeth loved fairies, "At the bottom of the garden, where the sun always seemed to be shining, is 'The wood' - the haunting of fairies, with its anemones and ponds, and where the two ring-doves, Caroline Curly-Love and Rhoda Wrigley-Worm contentedly coo in their wicker-work Ideal Home."

This secret hide out was set with untarnished nostalgia into the genial little world created by Elizabeth at St Paul's Walden Bury.

Mother had the loveliest ideas in the world, and she would read endless fairy stories to Elizabeth and David at bedtime.

The Magic Circle

The weather is warm and sunny. Elizabeth and David run past "The Bounding Butler" to the bottom of the garden, near the pond. "Shhh David . . . If we go down gently on our hands and knees . . . we may be lucky to see fairies today."

David bent over the pond and could only see his own reflection in the clear water, tiny goldfish swam about making little round ripples on the surface of the water.

Elizabeth said . . . "You have to close your eyes, make a wish, as mother said, they are only little spirits. They live in blossoms, amongst the dew in grass under mushrooms and leaves and in the trees! If you wish hard enough you will see them."

David listened . . . then he shut his eyes tight . . . he thought . . . "Elizabeth is always right".

Then . . . tiny little fairies and elves danced in front of him in circles.

Then . . .

A silly old frog, sitting on a lily pad . . . croaked . . . and David opened his eyes. He found Elizabeth creeping all over the lawn looking for four leaf clovers . . . When will she ever stop?

"I've found it!" she exclaimed.

Bobby The Bullfinch

Bobby and Elizabeth were good friends. A bullfinch is a beautiful bird, he can be taught to speak, sing simple tunes and is easily tamed. With its soft piping sound resembling 'wheeb' the bird composes 'teek-teek-tioo'.

It loves living in cornflour fields that have dense undergrowth both in lowlands and in mountains, overgrown parks and large gardens. It loves berries and, in early spring, devours flowering trees, especially fruit trees, which makes gardeners keep a watchful eye on their plantations.

Elizabeth allowed Bobby out of his cage and during meal time in the nursery he would fly to Elizabeth, perch beside her on the table and feed off her plate.

Bobby was a good obedient bird that Elizabeth would summon back to his spacious cage giving him fresh seeds and water. He would gladly return to his own home and would then warble gently in soft tones.

A Destiny Unfolds

Our fantastic journey makes us rise above the rooftops of London. We see Buckingham Palace, Big Ben, the Houses of Parliament, the Albert Hall and the Thames River. An exciting event is about to take place . . .

Montague House London

The time traveller brings us to this beautifully prepared festivity, we mingle with the children, play exciting games, eat tasty cookies, cakes and sweets. The Duchess of Buccleuch was to give a birthday party, with the excitement of a conjuror performing magic, entertaining the little group of Edwardian children.

The setting was magical for a great party, maybe Elizabeth's best party yet.

The Birthday Party

Lady Elizabeth's family house in London was number 20 St James's Square. She was very well liked and was always invited to children's parties. At this particular child's birthday party unknown to Elizabeth, she would meet her future husband.

This was the ten year old second son of the Prince of Wales and Princess Mary, the future King and Queen of England, and grandson of the reigning King Edward VII. With expressive sapphire blue eyes she looked at Albert, finding him alone at the side of the room.

"Hello, do you like riding?" Elizabeth asked, "I have a pony called Bobs and a bullfinch called Bobby. Do you like animals?"

"Yes," Albert replied.

Prince Albert
The Royal Navy was
always his chosen career.

They were soon conversing together. Albert was very impressed by Lady Elizabeth's confidence, his instant fondness made him feel comfortable to be in her company.

"Don't go away," Albert said.

"I won't if you want me to stay," Elizabeth answered reassuringly.

Elizabeth was kind and to make Albert feel at ease she removed the cherries from her cake, and as a gesture of friendship she slipped them onto his plate.

"These cherries are delicious, you can have them."

This must have made Frederick Arthur George very happy to have found such an instant friendship. They remained partners in all games until Elizabeth's nurse came to fetch her, she held out her hand to Albert and in a gesture she had seen mother make, and in her best manners said,

"Goodbye. I expect I shall see you again."

Then, as an afterthought, "What is your name?"

"Bertie," he answered.

"And mine's Elizabeth."

Sunny Days

MARIALUISA.

O ur 'Time Traveller' could not find more of a majestic landscape than one would find in Scotland. It can be bitterly cold, but today being summer the reflected light from the mountains and lakes creates an awe inspiring atmosphere.

Red Indians

Racing through the vast gardens towards the village with home-made bows and arrows slung on their shoulders, painted faces, feathers on their heads, a minute red Indian chief and his squaw would raid the quiet Scottish village.

They would see who they could capture and tie up with string to some of the railings in front of the quaint shops.

Picnic days and wild flowers.

They picnicked under the cool trees and after the meal they would search for flowers and herbs - stonecrop, speedwell, herb-bennett and bulge, marjoram and myrrh were picked to Elizabeth's delight.

After tea they would visit the tenant farmers on the estate. Farm life, the crops, and their animals, made Elizabeth understand the people and the different things they had to do.

Elizabeth and David met up with her father's forty-five year old factor.

"How do you do Mr Ralston, I haven't seen you look so well, not for years and years, but I am sure you will be sorry to know that Lord Strathmore has got the toothache."

Behind The Green Baize Door

Elizabeth and David were feeling rather hungry. "The pantry could be good . . . " thought Elizabeth. She always took the lead and they went quietly down the stairs. The smells of the delicious creams, chocolate cakes and delicacies prepared for the guests invited for tea were kept behind the green baize door!

"Shhh . . . now we can knock on the door!" Elizabeth remarked, "Mrs Thompson will surely give us something nice."

Mrs Thompson looked at the two little ones in admiration.

"And what can I do for you two?"

"May we come in Mrs Thompson . . . Could David and I have some of those nice cream cakes?"

The housekeeper could not resist their request, she thought they were the dearest little couple she had ever seen.

Two stillroom maids worked all day making the delicious confectioneries for the big traditional Scottish teas.

On this particular day, it was raining heavily, Elizabeth and her brother ran down to the still room and went straight to Mrs Thompson. The freshly baked buns, scones and cakes looked good enough to steal, and the bread smelt deliciously inviting.

"May we make our own little buns from the dough today? I could make a ginger bread man or a ginger bread pig, with currents for the eyes. And David could help me! Please . . . please" Elizabeth said in her best convincing voice.
With patience Mrs Thompson taught them how to make the cookies, and they baked them and would have a good treat indeed.

The Village Fair

The 'Time Traveller' leads us into crowds of village people enjoying the funfair. We may try our luck at the shooting gallery to win a bear or a doll, then eat doughnuts, lollipops and cucumber sandwiches.

The Raffle In The Vicar's Garden

The people came in crowds, a happy mood, the merry go round set, the musicians, the clowns and the food stalls were ready for a great day. Elizabeth and David were not quite in the happiest mood, for their pig, Lucifer, was given up for a raffle to raise money for the village church.

The people crowded the area where the little pig was the main attraction, Elizabeth and David sat next to each other cross-legged on the grass in the front row.

"Oh David . . . we only managed to buy half of the existing raffle tickets, I hope we win!"

Elizabeth had opened her money box, but the pennies saved were not enough.

They had begged everybody to give them some extra money so they could buy all the raffle tickets.

Unknown to them, this was not to be . . .

David said "Do you think we have a chance to win Lucifer back?"

"Shhhh David."

Elizabeth's mind was far too occupied to even hear what David was saying, she was already dreaming of taking Lucifer back home. The moment was never-ending.

The clown put his hand into the glass jar of the raffle tickets, pulling out the winning ticket.

"Oh no!" said Elizabeth, "Look, that man we don't even know has just got up to claim his pig . . . we shall never see poor Lucifer again!"

55

The Brew House

The 'Time Traveller' always allows us to pretend . . . Today . . . we will skip school and follow Elizabeth and her brother along the path of their secret walk to see where she will lead us . . .

56

The Brew House

As the six year old Elizabeth reached the back door with David tagging behind . . . they sneaked out of the house . . . today . . . they were going to miss lessons. Merry Mischief found secret walks, and enchanted places to play . . . she was in search for her next hiding place in the grounds.

They walked towards The Brew House.

"We can hunt for bantam eggs today" said Elizabeth. David sighed . . . they were always exploring and looking for something.

"I thought we could go into The Brew House today David."

"Are we allowed?" said David.

"No silly, don't you understand, we're pretending, you know . . . to have our very own secret house!"

The two children reached the brew house. It was the ruined outbuilding where the household ale once had been brewed.

Though dusty and full of cobwebs it was safe enough for the children. At that moment the first raindrops fell.

"Quick David, lets go in." Stepping into a rather dark, damp room Elizabeth discovered a rotten, rickety but sturdy enough ladder for them.

"It's safe!" she exclaimed.

Being a remarkably knowing child she would carefully think out her plot and not take too much of a risk.

"It's an attic!" she exclaimed as up they both climbed. "Look David, our very own blissful retreat, what a lot of room up here! . . Allah . . . will never find us up here . . . I've found the perfect place for us . . . imagine . . .

. . . nobody will ever find us here!

"She is a chatter box," David thought.

This was a little too much for him . . . he was still out of breath from climbing the ladder, he could hardly keep up with Elizabeth's adventurous energy.

Elizabeth took his hand reassuringly, she smiled down at him, "Oh! Little brother." She sat him down comfortably on a dusty heap of hay and out of the pocket of her rumpled frock came out . . . two apples and a slab of chocolate Meunier which she had earlier slipped out of the kitchen pantry.

"Can you keep a secret? . . David? . . David!"

David looked up at his sister in admiration . . .

"Yes!" he said in a small voice.

The days that followed were difficult . . . the Edwardian staff were extremely grand . . . footmen, factors, cooks, valets, ladies, maids, bootblacks and chambermaids, coachmen, grooms and stablemen, parlour-maids, nurses, gamekeepers, stalkers, ghillies, gardeners, gatekeepers, farm labourers, carpenters, stonemasons, nannies, governesses, nursery maids and more!

The two Benjamins had to enter the brew house without being seen. They walked carefully . . . Elizabeth wanted the attic to be their very own. Bringing forbidden delicacies from the pantry . . . sweets, chocolate Meunier, biscuits, sugar, apples and oranges and packets of Woodbines.

One sunny morning, Elizabeth planned to escape the morning's lessons. She hurried David to the Brew house, by then Allah was a little worried where the two had got to. Unknown to Elizabeth, a search party was organised.

Suddenly the rain came pouring down . . . and the little ones could not return home to the main house, perhaps it would clear up by the afternoon.

"Oh!" Elizabeth said "This is pretty irritating . . . I wish so hard that the rain should stop." Allah guessed the guilty pair could be hidden in the "Flea House."

Mother led the way.

Reaching the outhouses of The Brew House, the frantic hour long search stopped. Mother and Allah found the two. The rotten ladder was a death trap for any grown-up to climb.

"Come down Elizabeth!" Mother ordered. Elizabeth's grubby cheeky little face looked down . . .

"Don't worry mummy! . . We won't do it again!"

Elizabeth knew instinctively she had lost her blissful retreat. Mother was too relieved to be angry, while the Two Benjamins, safely came down the dangerous ladder. Mother hugged them both!

Elizabeth and David adored her. Although loving, Lady Strathmore expected the highest standards from her children. She was not lax in her dominant personality. She had a fine way of teaching her children.

The rain stopped and the sun was shining once more, mother tried being cross with Elizabeth, but she was far too charming with ready answers, and her instinctive sense of right and wrong.

Elizabeth would kiss mother on the cheek,

"After all mother it was only a bit of fun."

The secret den was now out of bounds for ever and the two were put to bed.

Protectors of Glamis

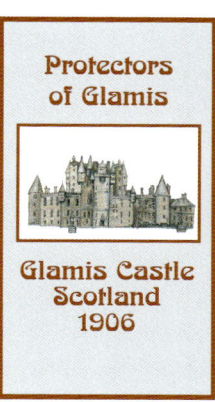

The 'Time Traveller' brings us inside Glamis Castle. The two adventurous little children would have endless exploring to do, through the labyrinth of passages, secret staircases and chambers. Let us follow them through the narrow twists and turns and see where their journey takes them . . .

60

The Protector of Glamis

The Countess, Lady Strathmore, was forty when she had a handful to rear in the Two Benjamins. "Elizabeth and David, please go and wash up, brush your hair and ask Allah to put clean clothes on you, the guests will soon be arriving for tea."

Always surrounded by high spirited adults, Elizabeth grew up remarkably fast for her age, with well developed social skills but never lost her sense of fun and imaginative zest for mischief.

The Ancient Battle and Siege

"David!" Elizabeth said with eyes wide open,

"We must defend and protect Glamis Castle today! . .

Imagine . . .

Mother has invited more invaders for tea!"

As usual her plan worked quite well and seemed to be great fun. Carrying a bucket of cold water up the winding steps of the castle's topmost tower, was not an easy task, but Elizabeth's determined nature kept the two climbing up the never-ending narrow steps.

"Now then David! I shall turn this water into boiling oil . . .

you know . . .

like in the medieval times!"

61

From the top of the turret, Elizabeth asked David to help her lift the heavy bucket of water onto the ledge. They tipped the bucket of water onto the intruders below.

"Oh no!" The visitors exclaimed.

Taken by surprise and looking up to see who was up there, ninety feet up, Elizabeth and David, ducked down and could be heard giggling.

"Quick David . . . lets go down to our room, Allah will be after us and telling mother."

They were safe in their rooms and the little lads loyal silence made it easy for Elizabeth to think up her next imaginative move.

Garden of Serenity

A garden of splendour and visual delights,
a gentle contoured land,
a view of nature's unique sight,
conducted by Almighty hand.

The suns dips its rays,
on the sparkling drops of the early morning dew,
Painting a spectrum of multiple tone,
tingled with golden hew.

Where peace and harmony grow side by side,
and the fields of memory do please,
where every flower opens and stands with pride,
reminiscing the past with ease.

The music in trees,
when the wind blows the leaves,
a breeze in butterflies, birds, bugs and bees,

it is to see love of nature in pure alchemy,
for this is the garden of serenity.

*Always surrounded by high-spirited adults, Elizabeth
grew up remarkably quickly for her age*

*"Shall us sit and talk"
Elizabeth would corner a guest and hold their
attention for hours*

The wheel of time spins endlessly on.
Beyond the light in Heaven's vault,

Hark! the gentle music of angels song,
among the stars infinity, a never ending place
void of strife.

Prompts a message of eternal life.

65

Bible Stories

Mother read the Bible to Elizabeth and David, she told them the story of Joseph and his little brother Benjamin, the youngest of the tribe . . . The 'Time Traveller' is journeying back into the land of Israel . . .

Joseph & His Coat Of Many Colours

Joseph was so fearless and honest, bright and clever, he followed the way of truth. He could explain the meaning of dreams, a gift that was given to him surely by God. One night Joseph had a strange wonderful dream . . .

"Behold, we were binding sheaves in a field and low! My sheaf arose, and stood up-right! And, behold, your sheaves stood up, too, all around and bent down before my sheaf!"

This showed that Joseph was to become a leader in his family and that one day he would be able to protect them all. He understood this in the right way, because he had a just and warm hearted nature. His father, Jacob, loved him in a special way, but his eleven older brothers were jealous of this. One night Joseph had a second dream. He dreamt he was all alone, travelling through a deep blue sky . . . the sun, the moon and eleven stars revered him. Could he become a mighty chief?

Joseph's father, Jacob, gave him a most beautiful coat of many colours, this made the other brothers very jealous.

His father sent him to the pastures in Shechem, but when he arrived he found there were no flocks. He met a solitary wanderer by the well, who was able to tell him that his brothers had taken the flocks to new feeding grounds.

He heard the lowing of the cattle and the soft bleating of sheep. When he found his brothers he ran forward to greet them, but they hated him and his kind nature, and were not pleased that he had found them. They stripped his beautiful coat from his shoulders and threw him into an empty pit nearby.

But when the Ishmaelites passed in a long procession of camels, Judah suggested they sell Joseph as a slave for twenty pieces of silver. So the young son of Israel was taken away, and when they reached Egypt, they in turn sold him to a rich man called Potiphar, who was an officer under Pharaoh, the Great Egyptian King.

Jealousy and a false story was told to Potiphar about young Joseph . . . that he was put into the King's prison. But the way of truth and trust in God, enlightened Pharaoh and he sent for Joseph, pardoned him and gave him his old place with Potiphar in the royal household.

Pharaoh knew of Joseph's talent of interpreting dreams, Joseph was called before the mighty ruler of Egypt, and Pharaoh asked him to interpret his curious dream.

Pharaoh saw seven fine fat cows feeding in the meadow, then out of the river came seven thin cows and they ate all the fat cows. Then a stork of seven ears of corn, and then another stork with seven thin ears. The thin ears ate all the fat ears up. Joseph's interpretation was this;

"Both dreams are one, God has shown the Great Pharaoh there shall be first seven years of plentiful harvest in Egypt, then seven years of famine. The harvests should be stored up in the good years ready for the days of want, God has shown you the way."

Pharaoh placed his own ring on Joseph's hand and put a gold chain round his neck, and Joseph was given the power to store up the harvests during the seven years of plenty. His ten brothers came to buy corn, they bowed down to the brother they once so cruelly treated and sold, just as the sheaves of corn had bowed down in Joseph's dream so long, long ago. The famine was very bad in Canaan, the brothers had no idea that this splendid man dressed like an Egyptian was their brother they had sold to the Ishmaelite long ago. Joseph pretended to mistrust them and questioned them about Benjamin their younger brother and would not sell them anything at all until they would bring Benjamin to him.

They went away and Joseph had put all their money back in the top of their sacks of corn. The brothers returned with Benjamin as promised. Joseph, prepared a banquet for them, he went away for a short while to weep for love and joy.

When the brothers went away with their corn, Joseph had again put their money back into the tops of their sacks, but in Benjamin's sack, he put not only money, but his beautiful silver cup.

He sent the servants to find his stolen silver cup, though they did not know that Joseph had put the cup there himself, and commanded them to find the one who stole the cup and to bring him back to be his slave.

Behold! The cup was found in Benjamin's sack.

Judah begged that Benjamin should be released and offered to become his slave instead.

Then Joseph revealed his true identity and told his brothers that he was Joseph the son of their own father, Jacob of Israel.

He bade them to fetch their father and with great happiness and joy, Jacob now very old, embraced his son Joseph and then was presented to the mighty King of Egypt.

Pharaoh was fair and gave the children of Jacob the land of Goshen, where corn fields and palm trees stood near the river Nile, flowing through the meadows. The land of Goshen now belonged to the Israelites and their children and their grandchildren for many years to come.

69

The Haunting
lost in time ...

All of a sudden the 'Time Traveller' has lost its way.

The clock strikes midnight and stops, time moves neither forward nor backward.

We are in the twilight of Glamis . . .

The moon prompts our imagination to visualise eerie ghostlike shapes . . . ravens, bats and owls fly around the tall turrets of Glamis . . . The castle is steeped in legends . . . Shakespeare is said to have been inspired by Glamis Castle for the setting of his famous play Macbeth . . .

Supernatural

It was a cold Autumn evening, the wild wind was blowing around the tall turrets. In the older parts of the castle legends have been created and handed down about Supernatural sightings.

But the history of the ghosts were reported as all being friendly, so most of the time the children were untroubled by its sinister reputation.

The castle is chilling in the blue room . . . Lord Halifax commented that 'Beardie Crawford', in 1486, quarrelled over a game of cards. He would carry on playing cards with the devil, if he wanted to, forever.

In the dark, the shadowy forms came and went through the dimly lit flicker of candle light. With the play of the imagination, walking through the gloomy passages and staircases would give you an eerie sensation.

The Unknown

Elizabeth told mother she met a strange white lady in a long dress, she smiled at Elizabeth . . . but never spoke, then passed her by. Mother reassured her there was no harm done and not to be afraid.

This gave Elizabeth strength not to be afraid of spirits or ghosts, so that later on when guests spoke about the supernatural she would play a game to frighten them. Mother said "Go to bed children, and I will see you in the morning."

But David suddenly remembered that he had left his storybook in the Crypt . . . he was afraid because his imagination had caused him on many occasions late at night to see shadowy people.

"Mother!" David exclaimed "I don't want to meet those grey people again . . . could a footman accompany me?"

"Certainly not" said Lady Strathmore firmly, "You have to understand there is nothing to be afraid of, you don't need anyone to take you, you must go by yourself."

David went pale, but with mother's strong character he resigned himself and left the room.

Elizabeth slipped out of the room at the very same time and holding out her tremulous hand, she whispered in his ear . . .

"Mother said, you were not to ring for someone to go with you but she didn't say you couldn't have me."

Hand in hand the two little shadows set off to brave the unknown.

David found his book, and Elizabeth's brave maternal instinct and protectiveness banished his fears away. Although she herself was not quite sure of the realms of the supernatural stories of the castle.

After all she was only twenty one months older than her "darling bruvver."

Velasquez
The Infanta Margarita.
circa 1655–1656
Kunsthistorisches Museum, Vienna

Velasquez

Imagine dressing up . . . it makes us change out of the times we live in. The 'Time Traveller' leads us to the court of Philip the fourth of Spain . . . We walk the streets of Madrid, this is a day of festivity and joy . . . Make believe leads Elizabeth and David to join us . . .

Two big dressing up chests, kept in the crypt, filled with all sorts of exciting costumes; brocaded dresses, cloaks, hats, wigs, masks, fans, lengths of silk and velvet, in fact everything a child could need for a game of make-believe.

Velasquez

Lady Strathmore admired Velasquez and his paintings. Velasquez was blessed with a harmonious domestic life with children and grandchildren. He had a serious, reflective nature.

From his portrayal of beautiful children he painted at the court of Philip IV in Madrid in 1623,

Lady Strathmore was inspired to recreate the atmosphere of the court. With her "Two Benjamins" the young children would dance the minuet.

Mr James "Dancie" Neill the dance master taught them the exacting performance.

The distinguished guests were well entertained.

On a special occasion, the minister was totally transported by the children's performance, and noted;

"For one brief yet supreme half hour the seventeenth and twentieth centuries were one" he remarked.

The Strathmores had been the last family in Scotland to employ a jester, so David's beautiful jester's costume, complete with cap and bells, was chosen from the wonderful treasure chest containing a variety of costumes and wigs.

Lady Elizabeth loved dressing up in her long pink and silver brocade dress made by her mother to recreate the spellbound atmosphere of the court life Velasquez portrayed in his paintings.

Elizabeth adored being the centre of attention in a large party of adults, and when asked the name of the character she portrayed she simply said,

"I call myself the Princess Elizabeth."

The sunlit Italian garden overflowing with sweet smelling flowers and tall cypresses, brings a touch of Tuscany to the Scottish castle of Glamis.

MARIALUISA MARINO

Florence

We have just left London's 'mall', lined with beautiful flags. The grand procession is over and a multitude of well-wishers are going home. 22nd June 1911 was the memorable day of the coronation of King George V where, for a brief moment, Elizabeth saw her future husband . . . We are heading home and then . . . off to Florence . . .

Villa Capponi, Florence

Elizabeth, now ten, and David, nine, were to visit their maternal grandmother, Mrs Harry Scott, in Italy. Mrs Scott lived in the hills of Florence in Fiesole. This would be Elizabeth's and David's first foreign adventure. They were very excited about travelling on the scenic railway journey. From the seat of the train they could enjoy breathtaking views of the countryside, crossing valleys and villages.

heir spinster Aunt Violet would escort them, the train would take a legendary route through the ever changing landscape.

The journey started in London's Victoria station, then taking a boat train from Dover, crossing on the ferry to France and stopping at Calais. Then onto Paris 'Guard du Nord', boarding the Trans-Alpine Express onwards to Switzerland through the Simplon tunnel and their final destination - Florence!

It was exciting to hear . . . the hiss of the steam train and the metal clanking, then . . . the train was off . . . "Tickets please!" the inspector called in a friendly voice . . . Aunt Violet produced three tickets.

"You are going a long way!" the inspector exclaimed.

"Yes!" Elizabeth interrupted, with pride, "We are going to visit my grandmother Mrs Scott in Florence, she is ever so good to us!"

ith eager anticipation both children were looking forward to seeing their grandmother. Mother had equipped them with new summer clothes from Gorrings, complete with straw hats and summer bonnets.

"Don't you feel grown-up!" Elizabeth exclaimed, "Look, our very own sleeping compartment."

"The train is beautiful" David said. "Shall I sleep on the top bunk and you below?"

"If you wish!" Elizabeth said.

80

The children awoke to the trains rhythmical hissing and straining, "This morning, we will go to the restaurant car for breakfast, we can choose exactly what we want to eat. Just like when mother and father travelled together to London."

Aunt Violet was quite fun and was not quite as strict as Allah, the children were comfortable and relaxed with her . . .

Florence at last!

The sun was setting creating beautiful golden colours over the gentle hills of Florence. The two children and Aunt Violet found the chauffeur waiting for them at the station. The trunks and luggage were collected and organised into the back of the car.

Off they went in a happy mood, heading for the Tuscan hills, where grandmother Scott was awaiting them at The Villa Capponi.

They arrived a little tired from the train journey, but very excited.

The Capponi Villa has wonderful views of the city. The plain exterior of the turreted sixteenth century villa follows the curve of the road. The tall walls conceal a delightful interior, with one corridor leading to a long green lawn and a lemon garden, and another leading towards the vast terrace from which you descend to a walled garden. There are others beneath it, ending in a swimming pool edged by cypresses.

Built by Gino Di Lodovico Capponi, in 1572, whose heirs continued to enlarge and embellish the villa. Lady Scott, the daughter of the Duke of Portland, acquired it in 1882. She added two lodges which were built with reclaimed columns from the ancient market. This is where the present Piazza Della Republica stands today.

Marialuisa Marino

The butler opens the grand door, "Buona sera, benvenuti, entrate per favore!" After the Italian welcome, Aunt Violet and the children are shown to the freshly prepared and beautifully decorated rooms. There were toys and games for the children ready for them to play.

The villa was truly warm and gracious. When Aunt Violet and the children were freshened-up and changed, they were summoned downstairs to the dining-room for supper.

There, a smiling loving grandmother, as always, welcomed them with open arms.

The next morning, the children were awakened by the sounds of birds. They opened their window to the most lovely sunny summers day. Life was good!

Running down the stairs, as if they had always lived there, Elizabeth and David found Grandmother Scott in the morning room. This was a most inviting bright room; through a grand arch you could see into the next room. It had beautiful furniture, ornaments, books, embellished with many vases of sweet smelling freshly cut flowers.

There was a little chapel with the walls covered in red damask, a most stunning alter piece painted by Tommaso Di Stefano and other wonderful paintings.

After breakfast the children were allowed to explore the beautiful gardens of the villa. The delightful flower beds, with lemon trees and a rose garden, that was probably created for a secret message of love, in contrast to the tall Cyprus trees, classical statues and gurgling fountains.

With terraced stepping stones and garden stones and garden seats shaded by arched floral creepers the atmosphere gave a true Renaissance element of gracefulness, harmony and beauty to the estate.

The undulating lush lawns were inviting to Elizabeth and David, they ran freely, hopped, skipped and played catchers with each other.

They saw many colourful butterflies and listened to the nightingales that would sing all day.

During their stay in Florence Elizabeth and David would have educational visits to the Pitti Palace and the Boboli Gardens.

These were golden days.

84

Everything was in perfect harmony. Exploring Florence, which could be declared as one of the most beautiful cities in the world, is rich in art. Aunt Violet would take the pair to The Uffizi Gallery, to see beautiful paintings and sculptures.

"Can we have refreshments at 'Doneys' Aunt Violet? . . after our tour . . ." Elizabeth asked.

The eight year old, Elizabeth, loved shopping too, she was enchanted by two winged angles dressed in real robes.

"How much? . ." she asked the stall holder. The man was so impressed in the way she bargained him down to three lire, a trifling sum.

"You may have the little angels, signorina, it is a pleasure to serve you!".

When Elizabeth finally ran out of pocket money a telegram was sent to her father: "S.O.S.L.S.D.R.S.V.P. Elizabeth."

Spring Am I

Spring am I,
in garlands fair,
rebirth I bring
in soil and air.

Spring am I,
so sweet my season,
where joy and life
bring forth good reason.

Spring am I,
my days that pass,
breathe hidden traces
of seeds in grass.

And when
my time
is ripe like grain,

I always will
return again.
Spring am I.

Four hundred and eighty miles back to Scotland.

Goodbyes

When we grow up time makes us remember what we used to do when we were little. Life becomes more of a responsibility and we have to cope with its trials set before us . . . Departing is always sad but we become stronger as we grow older and our memories will always be held in our hearts.

88

Goodbyes

Elizabeth loved London outings in Hyde Park, tea in the grand Houses of Mayfair, Belgravia and St James' and the gaiety of parties, but life was soon to change. David leaves home to attend a private school, Broadstairs, a feeder school for Eton, in the Autumn of 1912. Lady Elizabeth goes to the Misses Dorothy and Irene Birtwhistles day school in 30 Sloane Street, not far from the family home in 20 St James' Square in London.

"I shall miss you horribly darling Bruvver" Elizabeth said nostalgically.

"So will I" said David in a slightly more manly way.

Elizabeth spent only two terms as a day-girl at the London school, and even her French governess, 'Made' leaves the Strathmores service to get married.

Mother's adoring children often wrote to her:

To Mother: Elizabeth
My Darling Very Precious Loveable Love!,
I hope you had a very good journey, please give every kind of message to David. And do bring him up if you can. Lovie I was so sorry to have cried when you went away!

To Mother: David
Everything is very strange here and I feel very lost!

Elizabeth tried to comfort David by writing almost daily, to her "Darling Bruvver."

Elizabeth loved writing and showed a particular flair for English, winning a prize. She was an ideal pupil, scoring 30/30 for good conduct.

Kate Kubler, known as Miss Fraulein, was the Teutonic governess that mother engaged for Elizabeth. But a dramatic parting happened on the 10th of July 1914, less than a month away from the outbreak of the First World War. Elizabeth's kind-hearted and thoughtful nature would not neglect anyone that had helped her and she kept in touch with her old governess for many years.

Elizabeth always had perfect manners.

War

The large crowds went down the 'mall' and gathered outside the palace while King George V, now the nation's leader for four years, reluctantly announced the unavoidable news.

90

War

Lipunsky's dog, comedians, the jugglers Moran and Wise, the distinguished actor and producer Charles Hawtrey, the Russian ballerina Fedorovia, was a birthday treat from her mother, for passing all her Oxford examinations.

At the Coliseum in London on the night of Elizabeth's fourteenth birthday her childhood came to an abrupt ending. At eleven o'clock that night, King George V declared war on Germany. "It all seemed terribly exciting", Elizabeth would later recall.

The school room system collapsed completely. Elizabeth left London within a week. In Scotland she was installed in Glamis Castle, by now Glamis was converted into a hospital. The oak panelled dining room had been turned into a ward.

Lady Strathmore and Lady Elizabeth assisted in every possible way to make the soldiers feel at home. The wounded soldiers arrived in December and Lady Strathmore wished them to be treated as "honoured guests."

Christmas 1914, a giant christmas tree was set up in the crypt; the soldiers were dressed in hospital blue. Together with family, friends and those who volunteered to help handmade gifts and cards were exchanged.

This was Elizabeth's first Christmas at Glamis, as traditionally the family's festive gatherings were always at St Paul's Walden Bury. The unreality of the first months of war changed Elizabeth's life considerably. She was given responsibilities in the hospital at Glamis.

She became very thoughtful and conscientious for her young age, caring for others, giving many hours of her time, to nurse, run errands and post letters for the young soldiers. They in turn have never forgotten her, even our memories seen through the veil of time are still remembered with fondness.

rowing up was not easy, but her loving family gave her a balanced outlook on life. The modesty came from her father and the confidence and fortitude from her mother. She had the fabric and the determination to achieve greatness as she was courageous and dutiful. Elizabeth was on her way to a destiny with grace and charm that would make her one day a Queen.

The 'Time Traveller' Lands . . . Out Of Time

The ground shakes but it is only the sound of drums, is this war? The crowds run to the 'mall' toward Buckingham Palace . . .

Your heart is pounding as you run with them, your legs are tired . . . FASTER . . . FASTER . . . FASTER!

You want to get out of here . . . You run ever FASTER! . . . You run out of the crowds to . . . the edge of the book.

Your 'Out Of Time Traveller' is heading home to the safety of your own room. Your favourite teddy bear is still sitting in the corner where it always is . . .

Is it your imagination?

You thought you saw him wink at you . . .

94

Photographic portrait by Massimo Marino

95

N.D. Marialuisa Marino

*Accademia Internazionale Gentilizia
"Il Marzocco" Di Firenze constituita da Cosimo De
Medici nel 1446".*

*Marialuisa Marino is one of the outstanding artists of
her generation. The artistic challenge she relentlessly sets
herself in determination to break new ground, the
increasing number of private collections featuring her
work, together with the growing museum status, reflects
an obsessive dedication compelling respect."*
Bill Hopkins, International Association of Arts Critics.

*Unione Europea 2000
Titolo Onorefico Di Cavaliere dell'Etruria for the
portrait of Queen Elizabeth The Queen Mother
26 November 2000*

*Marialuisa has been awarded the 'Diploma Belle Arti e
Letteratura' Citta Di Catania, April 2001.*

BIBLIOGRAPHY

Alice, HRH The Duchess of Gloucester, Memoirs, (London 1983)
Aronson, Theo, Princess Alice, Countess of Athlone, (London 1981)
Aronson, Theo, Royal Family Years of Transition, (London 1983)
Aronson, Theo, The Royal Family at War, (London 1993)
Asquith, Lady Cynthia, The Duchess of York, (London 1937)
Barrow, Andrew, Gossip 1920-1970, (London 1978)
Barry, Stephen, Royal Secrets, (New York 1985)
Barry, Stephen, Royal Service, (New York 1983)
Barstow, Phyllida, The English Country Houseparty, (London 1989)
Beaton, Cecil, Self Portrait with Friends, (London 1979)
Bloch, Michael, The Duke of Windsor's War (London 1982)
Boothroyd, Basil, Philip, (London 1971)
Bradford, Sarah, George VI, (London 1989)
Buxton, Aubrey, The King in his Country, (London 1955)
Carol, Valerie, From Belfast's Sandy Row to Buckingham Palace (Cork 1994)
Churchill Papers, Churchill College, Cambridge
Colville, Lady Cynthia, Crowded Life, (London 1963)
Corbitt, F J, My Twenty Years in Buckingham Palace, (New York 1956)
Cornforth, John, Queen Elizabeth The Queen Mother, (London 1996)
Coward, Noel Diaries, (London 1982)
Crawford, Marion, The Little Princesses, (London 1950)
Dale, John, The Prince and the Paranormal (London 1986)
De Courcy, Anne, The Last Season, (London 1989)
De-la-Noy, Michael, The Queen Behind The Throne, (London 1994)
Dempster, Nigel, Princess Margaret, (London 1981)
Dempster, Nigel, Diaries of Sir Henry Channon, (London 1967)
Donaldson, Frances, King Edward VIII, (London 1974)
Dorling Kindersley, Chronicle of the Queen Mother, (London 1995)
Duchess of Windsor, The, The Heart Has Its Reasons, ' (London 1956)
Duff, David, Elizabeth of Glamis, (London 1971)
Duff, David, George and Elizabeth (London 1983)
HRH The Duke of Windsor, A King's Story, (London 1951)
Edwards, Ann, Matriarch, London 1984)
Forbes, Grania, My Darling Buffy, (London 1998)
Gathorne-Hardy, Jonathan, The Rise and Fall of the British Nanny, (London 1972)
Heald, Tim, The Duke: A Portrait of Prince Philip, (London 1991)
Hoey, Brian, Mountbatten, (London 1988)
Howell, Georgina, In Vogue, (London 1991)

Julian, Philippe, Edward and the Edwardians (London 1967)
Lacey, Robert, Majesty, (London 1977)
Lane, Peter, The Queen Mother, (London 1979)
Longford, Elizabeth, Queen Elizabeth The Queen Mother, (London 1981)
Lurie, Alison, The Language of Clothes, (London 1998)
Mabell, Countess of Airlie, Thatched with Gold, (London 1962)
Maclean, Veronica, Crowned Heads, (London 1993)
Massie, Robert K, Dreadnought, (USA 1992)
McDowell, Colin, One Hundred Years of Royal Style, (London, 1985)
McKee, Mrs The Royal Cookery Book, (London 1983)
Menkes, Suzy, The Royal jewels, (London 1985)
Menkes, Suzy, Queen and Country (London 1992)
Morrah, Dermot, The Royal Family in Africa, (London 1947)
Morrow, Ann, The Queen Mother, (London 1984)
Mortimer, Penelope, Queen Elizabeth The Queen Mother, (London 1995)
Nicolson, Harold, King George V, (London 1952)
Noblesse Oblige, Our Old Nobility, (London 1879)
Oliver, Charles, Dinner at Buckingham Palace (New York 1972)
Payne, Graham, My Life with Noel Coward, (London 1994)
Popc-Hennessey, James, Queen Mary, (London 1959)
Rhodes-Jarnes, Robert, Chips: The Diaries of Sir Henry Channon, (London 1993)
Roberts, Andrew, Eminent Churchillians, (London 1994)
Rose, Kenneth, King George V, (London 1983)
Ross, Josephine, Royalty in Vogue, (London 1989)
Salisbury, Marchioness of, The Gardens of Queen Elizabeth The Queen Mother, (London 1938)
Sinclair, David, Queen and Country, (London 1979)
Sitwell, Osbert, Queen Mary and Others, (London 1974)
Sitwell, Osbert, Rat Week, (London 1986)
Strong, Roy, Royal Gardens (London 1995)
Talbot, Godfrey, Queen Elizabeth , Queen Mother, (London 1989)
Townsend, Peter, Time and Chance (London 1978)
Tweedsmuir, Susan, The Edwardian Lady, (London 1966)
Wakeford, Geoffrey, Thirty Ycars a Queen, (London 1968)
Warwick, Christopher, King George V1 and Queen Elizabeth (London 1985)
Wentworth Day, Jarnes, The Queen Mother's Family Story (London 1967)
Wheeler-Bennett, Sir John, Kin- George VI, (London 1958)
Zec, Donald, The Queen Mother, (London 1990)